AR PTS: 2.0

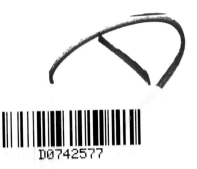

VAMPIRES™

TRANSYLVANIA: BIRTHPLACE OF VAMPIRES

Robert Z. Cohen

rosen publishing's
rosen
central®

New York

To Jack and Marge, my parents,
and to Pam and Ron, who pilfered my coin collection

Published in 2012 by The Rosen Publishing Group, Inc.
29 East 21st Street, New York, NY 10010

First Edition

Library of Congress Cataloging-in-Publication Data

Cohen, Robert Z.
Transylvania : birthplace of vampires / Robert Z. Cohen. — 1st ed.
   p. cm. — (Vampires)
Includes bibliographical references and index.
ISBN 978-1-4488-1228-8 (library binding)
ISBN 978-1-4488-2231-7 (pbk.)
ISBN 978-1-4488-2234-8 (6-pack)
1. Transylvania (Romania)—History—Juvenile literature. 2. Transylvania
(Romania)—Social life and customs—Juvenile literature. 3. Vampires—
Romania—Transylvania—Juvenile literature. 4. Folklore—Romania—
Transylvania—Juvenile literature. I. Title.
DR280.C64 2012
949.8'4—dc22
                                                          2010016106

Manufactured in Malaysia

CPSIA Compliance Information: Batch #S11YA: For further information, contact Rosen Publishing, New York, New York, at 1-800-237-9932.

On the cover: This is a picture of the Bran Castle in Romania, which is commonly known as Dracula's Castle.

CONTENTS

INTRODUCTION

"**I** have always been happy to invent mythologies for my birthplace," wrote the Transylvanian author Andrei Codrescu in his book *The Hole in the Flag*. "My motto: to a place rich in myth, add more." Already wealthy in culture and history, the real Transylvania is often obscured by the popularity of its most famous fictional inhabitant, the vampire Count Dracula.

Ever since the Irish writer Bram Stoker chose Transylvania for the opening scenes of his 1897 novel *Dracula*, the world has linked Transylvania with vampires, werewolves, and other scary creatures of the night. Many people are surprised to learn that a place called Transylvania actually exists. Transylvanians are often just as surprised to learn that many people think that their homeland is a fictional creation filled with monsters.

Transylvania is a large region located in the northwestern part of the Eastern European nation of Romania. It is home to a rich mix of ethnicities, each contributing their history and folklore to a fascinating cultural tapestry. Transylvanians maintain their folkloric traditions to this day. These traditions reveal the complex ways in which

people relate to life and death, to reality and the
supernatural world, and to power and history.

Truth is often stranger than fiction. A
Romanian prince named Vlad Dracula really did
exist, but he was different from the vampire count
found in countless books and movies. While many
Transylvanians hold folk beliefs similar to those in movies
and books about vampires, these beliefs can actually have very different
meanings. In the novel *Dracula*, Count Dracula tells the character Jonathan
Harker, "We are in Transylvania: and Transylvania is not England. Our
ways are not your ways, and there shall be to you many strange things."

Once considered a poor backwater of Europe, modern Transylvania
is rapidly modernizing. Romania entered the European Union in 2004.
Tourists and visitors from all around the world flock to Transylvania to
visit its medieval towns, ancient villages, and vast unspoiled mountains and
forests. Many visitors come seeking to visit the sites associated with that
most famous of Transylvanians: Vlad Dracula. What they find is a beautiful
land with a fascinating history, filled with friendly people.

THE PEOPLE OF TRANSYLVANIA

TRANSYLVANIA is a region in northwestern Romania. A large European nation, Romania has different regions that are home to a number of distinct local traditions and cultures. Much of the history and culture associated with Transylvanian vampire folklore is shared with other regions in Romania and the neighboring countries of Serbia, Bulgaria, and Hungary.

TRADITIONS AND BELIEFS

Ruled by many different countries and empires, Transylvania has a stormy history. A number of different ethnic groups have settled in Transylvania, bringing their unique languages, customs, religions, and folk beliefs with them. The interactions between these people make the folklore of Transylvania a vibrant mix of history and mythology.

Once a province of the Roman Empire, and later the Hungarian Kingdom, Transylvania became part of Romania in 1918 after the defeat of the Austro-Hungarian Empire in World War I.

After the collapse of Rome in the fifth century CE, the Christian Church of Rome remained as the most important functioning institution of civilization in Europe. Rome was split into two empires with separate churches. The western, Latin-speaking Roman Empire, located in Rome, Italy, had the Catholic Church. The eastern, Greek-speaking Byzantium Empire, with its capital city Constantinople (known today as Istanbul), was centered in present-day Turkey. The Byzantine church was Eastern Orthodox Christian.

Following the fall of Rome, many older beliefs and rituals of the pre-Christian Greek and Roman religions continued to be passed on, particularly older beliefs about the boundary between the living and the dead. The Greeks believed in *lamia*, or female demon vampires that fed on the blood of young men. The Romans believed in *lemurs*, the angry wandering spirits of those who had not been properly buried. Over time, these beliefs melded, creating a frightening folklore that spread throughout the eastern region of the former Roman Empire.

Transylvania was balanced between the two great empires. Ruled by a Catholic Hungarian king, it had a large population of Romanian and Slavic peasants loyal to the Eastern Orthodox Church. Among the mostly illiterate peasants of early medieval Transylvania, belief in pre-Christian mythologies helped explain aspects of their lives that were not addressed by the church. While Christianity replaced the majority of the old superstitions, many of the peasants' beliefs about death—including the fear of undead souls returning as vampires—remained.

THE ETHNIC MAKEUP OF TRANSYLVANIA

Transylvania is an excellent example of a multiethnic region. Groups of people migrated from one area to another, empires rose and fell, and

Monuments to Dacian leaders, such as this one to King Decebal carved into the Carpathian Mountain cliffs along the Danube River, are common sights around Romania.

borders and boundaries changed, but Transylvania remained. In Transylvania, different groups of people live side-by-side, speaking different languages and practicing different beliefs. In the time of medieval kingdoms, loyalty to a king defined a nation. The king and his court often spoke a different language than his subjects, and the borders of his kingdom rarely reflected actual ethnic boundaries.

As a result, throughout much of southeastern Europe (a region often referred to as the Balkans), many areas have a population that is mixed by language, ethnic group, and religion. In Transylvania and the Balkans, many people are able to speak two or more languages in order to communicate with their neighbors. In some Transylvanian villages, it is not uncommon to meet people who use three languages daily!

Romanians

The vast majority of people in Transylvania are Romanians. Romanian is a Romance language and is closely related to Latin. Before the Roman conquest, Transylvania was inhabited by a people known as Dacians. In

ROMA IN TRANSYLVANIA

The Gypsies of Transylvania call themselves the Roma. Most of them still speak a language called Romani, as well as Romanian, Hungarian, or both. Originating in India, the Roma people migrated westward as a group, reaching Europe around 1000 CE. They established themselves as blacksmiths, musicians, and craftsmen, but they were often persecuted and enslaved. Today, most Roma are not nomads but work as market sellers, factory workers, craftsmen, and farm laborers. Roma women in Transylvania often make a living as fortune-tellers. Of the many Roma tribes known by their professions, the most widespread are the Kalderash, who are coppersmiths, and the Lautarii, who are musicians. Roma follow the religion of the majority of people where they live, but they maintain their own folk beliefs and customs, especially concerning the dead. Some Balkan Roma avoid hospital care due to a fear of Bibi, a vampirelike witch that eats blood. Bibi is said to live near hospitals, where there is always a steady supply of blood. Although the Roma face discrimination to this day, many Roma organizations work tirelessly to help better the lives of their people in modern Europe.

105 CE, the Roman emperor Trajan defeated the Dacian king Decebal and established Roman rule over Dacia, which lasted until 275 CE. The modern Romanian language derives from the spoken Latin language brought by these Roman soldiers. Soldiers over the age of forty were given a farm as a reward for their services to the emperor of Rome. Almost all of them married local Dacian women.

Throughout the Balkan Peninsula, Latin-speaking Roman settlements endured long after the fall of the Western Roman Empire in the fifth century CE. The inhabitants of these settlements were know as Vlachs. Many Vlachs were seminomadic shepherds who could move their families and flocks into the high and inaccessible mountains when danger approached. A great number of Vlachs found safe refuge in the mountains of Transylvania.

Many Vlach tribes lost their language and assimilated into the majority populations that settled the Balkans: Greeks, Serbs, Bosnians, and Croats. Over the centuries, Vlach folklore was adopted into different languages and became a foundation for many of the commonly held beliefs among different Balkan peoples.

The Hungarians

The second largest ethnic group in Transylvania are the Hungarians, who call themselves the Magyar (pronounced "Mahd-yar") in their own language. The Hungarians were skilled horsemen, and in 895 CE, they swept over the passes of the Carpathian Mountains into Europe and settled in Transylvania and the Danube River basin. When the Magyar king Stephen converted to Western Christianity around 1000 CE, he forced the Magyars

This statue of Hungarian king Stephen is located in Budapest, Hungary. The Hungarians called Transylvania "Erdély," which means "the land beyond the forest."

to settle and adopt the European feudal system, in which noble families ruled over taxed estates. The Kingdom of Hungary grew large and powerful and established a series of protected cities and castles in Transylvania.

A large subgroup of the Hungarians, known as the Székely people, lived in the mountains of Transylvania. The Székely (pronounced "sake-hay") were settled along mountain passes as guards against further invasion, and as such, they were exempt from feudal taxes and serfdom. In Bram Stoker's novel *Dracula*, Count Dracula himself claims to be a Székely.

Saxons and Germans

Faced with ongoing invasions, the Hungarian king Géza II invited Saxon Germans to settle the mountainous southern part of Transylvania around 1150. They brought with them a strong military tradition. The Saxon region includes the walled castle towns of Bran, Sibiu, Sighisoara, and Brasov, which figure in Dracula mythology related to the famous Prince Vlad Tepes. Some Saxon myths claim that they are the descendants of the children who followed the Pied Piper as he chased the rats away from the German city of Hamelin. During the years when Romania was a communist country (1947–1989), most Saxons emigrated to Germany. Today, many are again returning to their ancient homes.

Other Groups

Traveling around Transylvania, one hears an astonishing mix of languages that can change from village to village. Besides the larger groups

A fiddler entertains a peasant woman at a fair in the Bihor region of Transylvania. His fiddle is a *vioară cu goarnă*, which utilizes a resonator with a bugle horn to create a loud volume when played.

of Romanians, Hungarians, and Germans, Transylvania is home to many groups whose folk tales have contributed to vampire folklore. These include Ukrainians (called Hutsuls), Armenian merchants, Serbs, Bulgarians, and Slovaks. Jews were numerous in Transylvania until the Second World War, where many were killed in the Holocaust. Today, only a few thousand Jews remain in the region.

TRANSYLVANIAN HISTORY

MEDIEVAL Transylvania was a province of the Kingdom of Hungary, ruled by a Catholic Hungarian king who lived far away in the city of Esztergom, located north of Budapest, Hungary. To the south of Transylvania, the Romanians, Bulgarians, and Serbs were loyal to the Eastern Orthodox Christianity. After the Roman Catholic Church and the Eastern Orthodox Church split in the eleventh century, these two Christian religions coexisted in an uneasy peace.

In the fourteenth century, the Kingdom of Hungary—along with the rest of Christian Europe—was faced with the rise of the Ottoman Empire. The Ottomans were an Islamic Turkish people from Central Asia. They formed the western vanguard of the spread of Islam as they rapidly advanced into Southeast Europe.

ORDER OF THE DRAGON

In 1389, the Serb armies lost to the Turkish forces at the Battle of Kosovo. A possible Turkish invasion of Central Europe suddenly became a frightening reality. In response,

This Ottoman miniature shows a Turkish archer. Turkish nomads united under Sultan Osman and became known as Ottoman Turks.

nobles in Hungary created an international order of knights in 1408 that were pledged to fight to defend Christianity against Islam. It was called the Order of the Dragon. The patron saint of this order was Saint George, the dragon slayer. Among the eastern nobles initiated into the order was Duke Vlad II, the Voivode of Walachia. At this time, a Voivode was a ruler of a territory. As a member of the order, he took the Romanian title Dracul, which means "the Dragon."

Vlad Dracul's five-year-old son, Vlad III, was also taken into the Order of the Dragon and was known as Dracula, or "the Little Dragon." Born in the Transylvanian town of Sighisoara in 1431, Vlad III would become famous as one of the models for the fictional vampire Count Dracula.

VLAD THE IMPALER

The Kingdom of Walachia rebelled against the Hungarian King in 1415. In doing so, the Walachian princes accepted the protection of the Ottoman

Empire. They were allowed to continue to rule as Christians under Ottoman protection. This made them vassals of the Turkish sultan. To show his loyalty, Vlad II sent two of his sons, Vlad III and Radu, to the Ottoman Turks as hostages. When Vlad II was killed during a fight against the Hungarians in 1447, the Ottomans returned his son Vlad III to the Walachian throne.

In 1453, the Byzantine capital, Constantinople, fell to an Ottoman siege. The Christian kingdoms of Europe were shocked and terrified. The Turkish advance was stopped by Prince John Hunyadi of Transylvania, who formed an alliance with Vlad III. Hunyadi's forces defeated the Ottoman Army at the Siege of Belgrade in 1456.

After Hunyadi died in 1457, Vlad III rebuilt his Walachian kingdom. Vlad became suspicious of the disloyal noble families, known as boyars, who were responsible for the death of his father. On Easter Sunday, 1457, Vlad called a meeting with his nobles and their families. Vlad marched them to the mountain border between Walachia and Transylvania and forced them to build a castle perched dangerously on a high mountain ledge. Here, at Poenari Castle, hundreds of boyars died in forced labor. Those that survived were killed by impalement, meaning that a long stake was driven through their body. The stake was then planted in the ground for all to see. Soon, Vlad III became known as Vlad Tepes (pronounced "tse-pesh"), which means "the Impaler."

A REIGN OF BLOOD AND HORROR

Impaling enemies was an early, very effective form of military terror. Nobody mistook Vlad's message: if he could treat his own people this way, how would he treat his enemies? Vlad's reign of terror in Walachia was a warning to anyone who would contest his rule. His brutality would make the name Dracula live through history as a symbol of blood and horror.

This bust of Vlad Tepes is located in Sighisoara, Romania. Vlad Tepes is remembered in Romania as a brave leader who protected Europe from the Ottoman Empire.

Now firmly in control, Vlad allied himself with the new king of Hungary, Matthias Corvinus, the son of John Hunyadi. Together, they joined with the Pope in Rome in calling for a new crusade against the Ottoman Turks. When the Ottoman sultan Mehmet sent ambassadors to Vlad's court to collect the tribute tax Vlad owed, Vlad had the ambassadors' turbans carefully nailed to their heads and sent them back to the Sultan. When Turkish army units came to collect the tribute, Vlad had them impaled on stakes. The Sultan demanded a meeting. Vlad's response was to attack Turkish forces in Bulgaria and begin a campaign of terror against the Turks and their Bulgarian allies. In a letter dated February 11, 1462, Vlad wrote to the Hungarian king: "I have killed men and women, old and young . . . We killed 23,884 Turks and Bulgars without counting those whom we burned in homes or whose heads were not cut by our soldiers."

Sultan Mehmet sent an army of thirty thousand Turkish soldiers into Walachia in pursuit of Vlad. Vlad knew that the best way to dishearten his enemies was through fear. He retreated to the capital city of Târgoviste. When the Turkish Army arrived at Târgoviste, they were greeted by a horrific sight: twenty thousand Turkish prisoners had been impaled on stakes surrounding the empty city. The roads to the city were lined with the gory trophies for 60 miles (97 kilometers).

The angry sultan's forces finally surrounded Vlad at Poenari Castle, his mountain fortress. With the help of his trusted personal Roma guard, Vlad was able to escape and smuggle himself into Transylvania to seek the protection of King Matthias. Fearing a dangerous rival, King Matthias had Vlad imprisoned.

By now, Vlad was renowned in Europe for his success at stopping the Turkish advance and for his shocking cruelty in battle. He was a powerful bargaining chip in the Hungarian king's political struggle against the Ottoman encroachment into Europe. Vlad spent twelve years in Hungary, even marrying one of the Hungarian king's cousins, with whom he had two sons. The mere presence of the famed Impaler was a powerful tool in the deadly theater of diplomacy.

In 1476, Vlad was released to reclaim his throne in Walachia. With the help of the Hungarian king, he raised an army and fought to eject the Ottoman Turks. He was killed in battle near Bucharest; his head was cut off and taken to the sultan in Istanbul as proof that the famed Impaler, who had so shocked and terrified the Turkish armies, was finally dead.

Vlad Tepes may have been dead, but he wasn't finished. The legend of Vlad the Impaler began to grow almost immediately after his death. Russian

and German court scribes noted his success and chronicled his cruelties, and his legend continues to grow.

TRANSYLVANIA UNDER THE AUSTRO-HUNGARIAN EMPIRE

After the defeat of the armies of Hungary at the Battle of Mohács in 1514, the Ottoman Empire reached its apex in Europe. The princes of Transylvania wisely made a separate peace with the sultan and accepted the status of vassal state. In exchange for loyalty to the Ottoman Empire, the Transylvanians were allowed to rule themselves and practice their own religions without interference.

The Turkish advance westward was finally halted after the defeat of the sultan's armies at the Siege of Vienna (the capital of present-day Austria) in 1683. Hungary quickly fell to the Austrian Habsburg monarchy, and Transylvania followed in 1700.

Transylvania's tolerant atmosphere continued through the years of Habsburg rule, but in 1867, Hungary joined with Austria in a "dual monarchy,"

This Ottoman miniature shows the king of Hungary, John II Sigismund Zápolya, bowing before Ottoman sultan Suleiman. Zápolya signed the Edict of Turda in 1568, which established a tradition of religious tolerance in Transylvania.

also known as the Austro-Hungarian Empire. As part of this compromise, Transylvania lost its unique status as a separate country. Once again, it was fully absorbed into Hungary. The new Hungarian policy sought to assimilate other ethnic groups, upsetting Transylvania's long history of ethnic tolerance. Ethnic tensions grew within the Austro-Hungarian Empire until August 1914, when an angry Serbian nationalist assassinated the Habsburg Archduke Franz Ferdinand in Sarajevo, Bosnia, igniting World War I.

TRANSYLVANIA AND THE WORLD WARS

When World War I ended in 1918, the victorious French, British, and Americans hoped to finally settle the national conflicts of Europe. It was an impossible task. Ethnic groups and languages did not fit neatly into the new national borders that were drawn up. The multiethnic Austro-Hungarian Empire was dismantled. The Treaty of Trianon, signed in France in 1920, established Hungary's new borders. Although Hungary claimed Transylvania, it was awarded to Romania. Romania gained the entire region, as well as large minorities of Hungarians, Saxons, Jews, and Roma. The unification of Romania and Transylvania was celebrated in Romania, but it was seen as a tragedy in Hungary, and relations between the neighboring countries continued to sour.

As World War II dawned, Hungary made a pact with Nazi Germany to regain some of the lost territory in Transylvania. The Romanians, who were also allied with Germany at the time, felt cheated. Romania's support for Germany weakened, and the country finally switched sides to fight against the Germans. However, between 1941 and 1944, Transylvania suffered greatly under Nazi rule. Thousands of Transylvanian Jews and Gypsies were deported to the Nazi extermination camps.

THE VAMPIRE PRINCESS

The relationship between Transylvania and Habsburg-ruled Hungary was tested by the case of the bloody "vampire princess," Elizabeth Báthory. A daughter of the ruling Transylvanian Báthory family, Elizabeth married a Hungarian nobleman and moved to his castle in Csejte (today Čachtice in modern Slovakia). After her husband was killed in battle, Elizabeth lived in the castle alone. Local priests began to notice that the castle maids and noble handmaidens were disappearing at an alarming rate. Soon an investigation began, and Báthory was imprisoned. Between 1585 and 1610, she was said to have tortured and murdered as many as 650 young girls. This makes her one of the worst mass murderers of all time. Investigators claimed she sought eternal youth by drinking—and bathing in—her victims' blood. When she died in 1614, the fearful people of Csejte would not allow her to be buried in the village.

UNDER COMMUNIST CONTROL

With the arrival of the Soviet Union's Red Army, Transylvania was again unified with Romania. The Communist Party took control of the country, discouraging the ownership of private industry and property and collectivizing farms into state-run operations. Nicolae Ceauşescu became the prime minister of Romania in 1965. In 1974, Ceauşescu declared himself president of Romania and began to act as a dictator, throwing his critics

The harsh rule of Communist president Nicolae Ceauşescu brought misery to Romania.

in prison and following an economic policy that impoverished the once-rich nation.

Bread disappeared from stores, and eggs, meat, and milk became rare. Medicine became unavailable in hospitals. Life became a daily struggle to survive. Many Romanian historians think that Ceauşescu saw himself as a leader who was as fearsome as Vlad Tepes. Many others reviled Ceauşescu as a vampire, sucking the blood of the country.

The situation in Romania reached a crisis in the late 1980s, when Ceauşescu promoted the idea of "systemizing" villages. He began bulldozing villages into the ground in order to force the population to move to newly constructed apartment housing in cities. For Romanians, this was the last straw.

By 1989, as the other Communist nations of Eastern Europe had all peacefully begun to change to democratic government systems, Ceauşescu held on to power. In December 1989, a demonstration in the city of Timişoara turned into a general protest against the Ceauşescu regime. Ceauşescu's hated secret police, the Securitate, shot into the crowds, killing many. Soon, protests turned violent all over Romania. Ceauşescu and his wife, Elena, fled to Târgoviste, where they were arrested by the Romanian army, briefly tried for crimes of genocide and corruption, and executed. The long nightmare had ended. The "vampire" was finally gone.

CHAPTER 3

TRANSYLVANIAN VAMPIRES

HOW did Transylvania become fixed in the modern imagination as the birthplace of vampires? The answer can be traced to one man—the Irish author Bram Stoker. Stoker's 1897 novel *Dracula* remains the most successful vampire novel of all time. Besides influencing every vampire novel that followed it, *Dracula* changed the way people thought about vampires and Transylvania, a place that the book's author never actually visited.

BORDER LITERATURE

Europe's fascination with vampires grew during the years following the retreat of the Ottoman Empire in the Balkans. As the Austrian Habsburg Empire took control of formerly Ottoman territory, these areas became seen as the new frontier of Europe, a "Wild East" populated by strange people with strange customs. Austrian Army officers and government workers were soon writing popular books about their travels in these newly "discovered" lands. These books were called

This novella about Vlad Dracula was published in the early sixteenth century. The first stories about Vlad Dracula focused on his bloodthirsty reputation.

grenzeliteratur, or "border literature." *Grenzeliteratur* was similar in spirit to the Wild West novels published in nineteenth-century America.

The 1700s saw the spread of vampire reports throughout the Habsburg realm. The most famous of these early vampire scares occurred in 1727 in the village of Medvegia (today Medvedja), Serbia, which lies just west of Transylvania. A local soldier named Arnold Paole told villagers that he was a vampire but had cured himself by eating dirt from another vampire's grave. After his death, however, villagers claimed that Paole had risen from his grave and sucked the blood from four peasants. The villagers claimed that, after forty days, they dug up Paole's grave, and the corpse groaned when a stake was driven through his heart.

After reports of more attacks in 1731, villagers called in the Austrian military doctor Johann Flückinger to examine the bodies. His report filed in 1732, *Visum et Reportum* ("Seen and Reported"), became an immediate best seller. When the book was translated and sold abroad, it introduced a new word into both the English and French languages: "wampyre."

The Paole story became so popular that within a year, there were no less than twenty books published in German about "wampyres." The world's first vampire book craze had begun. In 1732, an English lord gave a speech in the British Parliament attacking his opponent as a "political Vampyre." By 1734, the German writer Michael Ranft wrote that, at the Easter book fair in Leipzig, "it was impossible to enter a bookstore without seeing something about bloodsuckers."

Soon, there were vampire hunters digging though cemeteries all over Europe, and their books sold fabulously well. In 1755, Empress Maria Theresa of Austria passed laws against the exhumation and destruction of corpses and other acts of superstition. Even the empress could not stop Western Europe's fascination with vampires, which satisfied people's need for exotic and scary new stories.

DRACULA AND FRANKENSTEIN SHARE A BIRTHDAY

Lord George Gordon Byron was a dashing young poet whose popularity in early nineteenth-century London was similar to that of a modern rock star. A poet, politician, and linguist, Byron was one of the leading figures of British Romanticism, a movement in which artists sought to describe extreme emotional states of love, horror, or awe.

In 1816, Lord Byron left England to settle in Switzerland. Some of his closest friends visited him there. These included the poet Percy Bysshe Shelley and his wife, Mary Shelley, and Byron's friend and personal doctor, John William Polidori. While visiting Byron at the Villa Diodati above Lake Geneva, they were kept indoors by a heavy rain. To pass the time, they entertained each other by reading from *Tales of the Dead*, a collection of French horror stories. Lord Byron suggested a ghost-story writing contest among the friends. Two of these stories eventually became world-famous Gothic novels. Mary Shelley turned her story into the 1818 Gothic novel *Frankenstein*. John Polidori later rewrote his story as the 1819 novel *The Vampyre*, which became the first English vampire novel.

The Vampyre is set in Greece, and the star of the book is the vampire Lord Ruthven, a romantic and mysterious noble gentleman hiding an evil secret. This dashing and noble Balkan vampire count would eventually inspire Bram Stoker's Count Dracula. In a sense, both Dracula and Frankenstein were both born from a night of ghost stories told in Switzerland.

BRAM STOKER

Born Abraham Stoker in 1847 in Dublin, Ireland, Bram Stoker was attracted to theater life and began his career as a theater critic at the *Dublin Daily Mail*, a newspaper owned by Sheridan Le Fanu, a writer of Gothic fantasy novels. Le Fanu published the popular vampire novella *Carmilla* in 1870. Stoker had a talent for writing, and soon his reviews attracted the attention of England's most respected theater actor, Henry Irving. Irving invited Stoker to move to London in 1878 and become the manager of the famed Lyceum Theater.

Few novelists have had as much influence on the perception of a place as Bram Stoker has on Transylvania. Although he had never visited the region, his fertile imagination would redefine Transylvania forever.

As secretary of the theater and Irving's personal manager, Stoker traveled widely around Europe and the Americas, meeting famous people and making important social connections. Stoker arranged many private parties for London's most interesting people to meet with Sir Henry Irving at the city's Beefsteak Club, a special reception room at the Lyceum. At these parties, Stoker befriended famous writers such as Sir Arthur Conan Doyle, the creator of Sherlock Holmes, and renowned explorers such as the Hungarian Arminius Vambery, who may have inspired Stoker to research the subject of Hungary and its mysterious province of Transylvania.

WRITING DRACULA

When not busy managing the Lyceum Theater, Stoker spent his holidays at the English seaside resort town of Whitby and used his time to write novels. Count Dracula was born in the summer of 1890—not in a

Transylvanian castle, but in the reading room of the Whitby town library. Stoker kept notebooks when collecting material for his novels, and in March 1890, he decided to write a vampire novel and call his main character Count Wampyr. Stoker first read about the legends of the historical Dracula in William Wilkinson's 1821 travel book *An Account of the Principalities of Wallachia and Moldavia*. Stoker made a note to himself: "Dracula in Walachian language means DEVIL."

Stoker began reading everything he could find about Transylvania in order to make his setting as realistic as possible. According to Stoker's careful notes, he dug deep into books about Transylvania's people and their superstitions. These notes also reveal that Stoker lifted entire passages almost word for word from the books he was reading about Transylvania, as well as from previously published novels and stories about vampires. Today, most writers would condemn this as plagiarism, but in the nineteenth century, it was a fairly common practice. Many modern scholars consider Stoker to have been a talented editor of the Dracula story, combining bits of the tale from different sources into an entirely new work.

Although Stoker used the name Dracula, he never mentioned

The Carpathian Mountains provided a rich backdrop for Bram Stoker's novel. Wild and unspoiled, these forests support Europe's largest population of wild wolves and bears.

the historical Romanian prince Vlad Tepes. Stoker's Count Dracula is a Székely (a Hungarian of the eastern Transylvanian mountains), and his castle is located in the Borgo Pass of the Carpathian Mountains.

Modern readers often find Stoker's *Dracula* a very difficult book to read. Although well received by critics, it was not an immediate best seller when originally published in 1897. Stoker's theatrical background and imagination made his tale a natural choice for a new storytelling device that was in its infancy when *Dracula* was published in 1897: the movies.

BELA LUGOSI

The 1931 film version of *Dracula* features a suave and dashing vampire count. This onscreen Dracula was the creation of Transylvanian-Hungarian actor Bela Lugosi. Born Béla Blaskó in the western Transylvanian city of Lugoj (his stage name means "from Lugoj" in Hungarian), Lugosi became an actor in Budapest. When Hungary lost Transylvania to the Romanian army after World War I, a new

Bela Lugosi, who was born in Transylvania and spoke with a thick Hungarian accent, made a very convincing Dracula. So convincing, in fact, that he acted in horror movies for the rest of his career.

1734-sp-19

109-131.

Hungarian Communist government was formed. This new government hoped that Russia, which had just had its own Communist revolution, would help in an effort to regain the lost territory.

Lugosi became a spokesman in the Hungarian Ministry of Culture. When the Hungarian Communist government was overthrown in 1919, Lugosi was forced to flee to America. He amazed American actors with his ability to memorize his lines phonetically in English—a language he did not yet speak. Lugosi had more success in silent film roles, where his lack of English did not hold him back. In 1927, he was chosen for the lead role in a Broadway adaptation of Bram Stoker's *Dracula*. With his thick Transylvanian-Hungarian accent—more goulash than ghoulish—and dark good looks, Lugosi was a natural for the 1931 film version of *Dracula*.

Lugosi was so good in the role, however, that he was forever after typecast as Dracula. Due to his strong Hungarian accent, he found it increasingly hard to get non-horror roles in films. A back injury led him to become dependent on painkilling drugs, and his behavior grew more erratic. By the 1940s, Lugosi was reduced to taking roles in less prestigious films. He had not lost his fans, however. When the aging actor checked into a hospital to treat his drug problems, singer Frank Sinatra paid all of his bills and came to visit him. Ed Wood, a director of strange movies that have since become camp classics, took pity on Lugosi and offered him vampire roles in films that had nothing to do with vampires. When Lugosi died in 1956, he was buried in the cape that he had worn in *Dracula*.

MODERN VAMPIRES

Many of the attributes that we associate with vampires derive from the nineteenth-century literature that reached its apex with Bram Stoker's

NOSFERATU

The first Dracula film was an obscure 1920 Hungarian silent film called *The Death of Dracula*. All copies of it have been lost. A year later, the German artist Albin Grau, who learned about vampires while serving as a soldier in Serbia in 1916, decided to film his own vampire story. Working with director F. W. Murnau, Grau began to adapt Stoker's *Dracula*. However, the two men did not have the permission of Stoker's widow, Florence Stoker, to use her husband's novel. Murnau and Grau went ahead anyway, changing the name of Count Dracula to Count Orlok and the title of the film to *Nosferatu*. They shot the film in Slovakia instead of Transylvania. Count Orlok was portrayed by actor Max Schreck as an ugly, rodentlike gremlin. Visually spectacular, *Nosferatu* premiered in Berlin in March 1922. Bram's angry widow sued the film company and won, and in 1925, the courts ordered all copies of the film *Nosferatu* to be destroyed. Luckily for film historians, some copies survived, and *Nosferatu* is now considered a classic of silent filmmaking.

Dracula. However, today's vampire stories are no longer strictly set in Transylvania and no longer closely follow the same rules. The TV series *Buffy the Vampire Slayer* (1997–2003) did away with Transylvania entirely and made an American high school the backdrop for contemporary vampire hunting. And when it comes to fear, even Transylvania cannot compete with high school.

TRANSYLVANIAN FOLKLORE: VAMPIRES AND MORE

THERE is a lot more to Transylvania's folklore than just vampires. Today, Transylvania is one of the few areas in Europe that has maintained traditional ways of peasant life into the twenty-first century. The majority of the population still lives in small villages, where modern conveniences such as indoor plumbing and telephones were slow to arrive. Horse carts are still a very common means of transportation. These communities have retained the tradition of telling stories on long, cold winter nights. Transylvanian folklore has been influenced by many different languages and cultures. It stresses beliefs and rituals that promote the well-being of families and the community as a whole. Nowhere is this more obvious than in how Transylvanians relate to the experience of death. Transylvanians, by and large, are very devout people, regardless of which church they attend.

THE HAPPY CEMETERY

In peasant cultures, the local community often has very set ideas about how to live and what comprises the

Rural Transylvanians continue to work their land using both ancient and modern methods. Horse carts do not require expensive fuel, and they are still widely used for transportation.

"right" way to do things versus the "wrong" way. The right way leads to prestige and esteem in the eyes of one's neighbors and, when death comes, a burial in a fine plot in the village cemetery. Villagers in Transylvania, as in many traditional cultures of the world, may have unique beliefs regarding where the border between the living and the dead lies. These beliefs and customs may seem strange to outsiders. For instance, in the village of Sapânta, located in the Maramureş region of northern Transylvania, the local graveyard is called the Happy Cemetery. Carved and painted wooden grave markers illustrate the lives of prominent villagers. The many churches in Transylvania flourish because they respect the unique beliefs and folklore of their members.

Transylvania was not always so tolerant. Membership in the Catholic Church was the mark of political loyalty to the Habsburg dynasty. In the 1700s, when the Catholic Habsburg Empire took control of areas with a Romanian ethnic majority, an agreement was reached with many local Romanian Orthodox churches. The Orthodox churches would accept political allegiance to the Catholic Church but were still allowed to maintain their traditional Eastern Orthodox rituals. However, Catholic priests spread the word that anyone not buried in a Catholic consecrated cemetery would be in danger of becoming a vampire. In areas under direct Habsburg control, such as Oltenia (just south of Transylvania) and Maramureş, there is still a strong tradition of vampire lore.

The Happy Cemetery is located in the village of Sapânta in the Maramureş region of Transylvania. The grave markers reflect a view of the world in which death is not an occasion only for sadness.

STRIGOI AND MOROI

The word "vampire" is unknown in the Romanian language. Instead, people speak about creatures such as the *strigoi*, *moroi*, *vârcolaci*, and *pricolici*. All of these figures display some of the characteristics we associate with vampires. For instance, almost all have the power to turn themselves into animal form. However, the word "vampire" means different things in different regions of Romania and Transylvania.

A common vampire figure is the *moroi*. *Moroi* are the mischievous souls of infants who died before being baptized in a church. They are most active around the Feast of St. Andrew (November 30), when people rub garlic around their doors and windows to protect their homes from evil spirits.

The most common vampire is the *strigoi*, a word that may derive from the ancient Greek *strix*, an evil bird spirit that fed on human blood. Strigoi are often believed to be the undead souls of somebody in the community who had unfinished business when he or she died; usually, the person acted strangely in life. The wandering souls of persons already buried are known as dead strigoi. Some people, however, are believed to be able to send their souls out to wander at crossroads at night. These people are called live strigoi, although this is also a common attribute of the *vrajitoare*, or a witch who has changed shape and acts like a strigoi.

Living strigoi are said to have two hearts and two souls and can send their malevolent spirit out at night to devour the blood of farm animals. It is said that the strigoi meet the moroi and vârcolaci at the boundaries of the village and together decide on their program of evil for the coming year, including which villagers they are going to kill. Elsewhere it is said that the dead strigoi meet with living strigoi at the village boundaries to teach them incantations and spells. When a person dies, his or her family takes great care that cats do not enter the room, for if a cat should walk over the body of the dead, the soul is in danger of becoming a strigoi.

FUNERAL RITUALS

It is believed that a person who has left unfinished business in life may be in danger of becoming a strigoi. It's common for the deceased's family to take ritual precautions to guard against this. In Maramureş there is a custom that is carried out when a young, unmarried person dies, called Nunta Mortului, or "The Wedding of the Dead."

The deceased person is believed to have a right to enter the next life as a full-fledged adult, so he or she must be married before burial. During the funeral service, the priest performs a wedding ceremony for the deceased, with a friend or volunteer standing in as the bride or groom. As one folk song says of this ritual, "It was not time for you to die, it was time for you to marry." It is believed that by performing this ritual in the church, the living can interact with the soul of the dead. This ensures that the soul of the deceased will find peace in being "married to God."

Romanians, like many other Orthodox Christian people of the Balkans, see the period immediately following a person's death as a time of transition when the dead person's soul lingers near those he or she left behind. Funeral rituals, such as the ritual feast called pomana, are held at the site of the grave so that the dead may be fed with a special white cake called coliva and wished a safe journey into the next world. The family holds a feast at the cemetery site each year, and the beautiful painted dishes used for the pomana foods are hung on the wall of the house as a keepsake to respect the departed.

The concept that the recently dead can respond to the living is also a part of the Hungarian folklore of Transylvania. In many villages (and especially among the Székely of the Carpathian Mountains), there are often old women in the villages who perform the function of *halottlátó*, or "death seer." A halottlátó can communicate with the souls of the recently departed.

In the Maramureş region of Transylvania, life revolves around the village church. More than forty log churches here date back to the fifteenth century.

THE CALUSARI: DANCING EVIL INTO GOOD

An example of how Romanian folk beliefs work in a positive manner to help people is found in western Transylvania and Oltenia. In some villages, groups of men gather with musicians every year on the fortieth day after Easter in a procession around the village. During this procession, they perform an ancient ritual drama called the *calusari*. The calusari ritual features a series of skits, songs and dances, and it is performed by all-male dancers, also known as calusari, to the accompaniment of folk musicians.

Port national de Călușeri

Young men who are training to become calusari are initiated into a secret ritual by a *vataf* ("master") who has inherited the knowledge of *descântece* ("magic charms") and the dance steps from his predecessor. The calusari are pledged to belong to the group for seven years. During this time, they are not allowed to enter churches. During the forty days following Easter, the calusari must avoid their wives and cover any mirrors in their homes so that they may not see their reflections. While dancing, they wear bunches of garlic on their belts to guard against evil spirits.

The calusari dance to ensure that their village has

The calusari tradition may come from an older religious belief system that predates the arrival of Christianity in the Balkans.

VÂRCOLACI: FEASTING ON THE SUN

In Transylvania, it is common to hear of vârcolaci and pricolici, malevolent shape-shifters who often take the form of dogs, wolves, or owls. The Romanian word *vârcolaci* is widespread throughout the Balkan region wherever vampire lore is found. The word has its origin in the Greek *vrykolaka*, a form of werewolf. Vârcolaci combine the behaviors of both vampires and werewolves.

Vârcolaci are not really considered dangerous to humans, but they bring bad luck when they appear. Vârcolaci are blamed for causing solar eclipses by eating the sun. During the solar eclipse in the summer of 1999, thousands of foreign tourists flocked to Transylvania, which was considered the best place in Europe to view the total eclipse. In the city of Cluj-Napoca, however, the streets were absolutely deserted as the hour of total eclipse approached. Some local Romanian fortune-tellers had predicted that the vârcolaci would be feeding on the sun, and many people preferred to play it safe and remain indoors.

Transylvanian villagers are still wary of wolves, which prey on herds of sheep on the mountainside pastures. They also take precautions against meeting the Fata Pădurii, or the "Maiden of the Woods." Much like the dryads of ancient Greek myth, these are spirits who live in the forest and try to lead handsome young shepherds astray. In some cases, the Fata Pădurii is recognized by the fact that she cannot speak Romanian.

a good harvest and is protected from malicious spirits. The calusari are able to protect the village from mischievous fairies known as *iele*. Iele are active at night, live outside of the village boundaries, and can cause illness. The calusari dance only during the day and only inside the village, have the ability to change the power of the iele from evil to good, and use this power to heal the sick. As they move through the village, the calusari stop to dance at the homes of sick people. Babies are brought to them, and the calusari dance over each infant to protect it from future illness. Today, the tradition of ritual calusari is kept alive by professional folk dance groups.

CHAPTER
5

MODERN TRANSYLVANIA

ROMANIA has come a long way from the dark times of the Communist era. Adapting to a free market system in the 1990s proved difficult, and many Transylvanians faced years of stark poverty. They looked for work in foreign lands, often traveling to Italy and Spain in search of jobs. Many Romanians were truly baffled to find that outside of their homeland, Transylvania was known as the land of Count Dracula. As more foreigners visited Romania, a new tourism industry boomed, bringing much-needed money into the local economies. Many of the new tourists were searching for vampires.

Transylvanians are famous for their hospitality and are always willing to please, so if the tourists wanted Dracula and vampires, then that is what they would get. Today, an entire industry caters to vampire-hunting tourists looking to retrace the footsteps of Count Dracula. Many such tours go to majestic Bran Castle, where Dracula may have been imprisoned briefly. A few tours even reach Vlad Tepes's own Poenari Castle, which still crowns an isolated mountain near the town of Curtea de Argeş. More

Even though historians are not sure if Vlad Tepes was ever really imprisoned in Bran Castle, it is a popular destination for tourists who go to Transylvania seeking Dracula.

historical Dracula territory is found in the beautiful medieval Saxon town of Sighişoara, where the house in which Vlad Tepes was born has been transformed into a Dracula-themed restaurant. The specialty of the house is steak served very, very rare. At one time, there was talk of building a giant Dracula theme park near Sighişoara, but it was decided that the city did not need any extra attractions to add to the flood of vampire tourism.

MODERN CASES OF VAMPIRISM

Old beliefs die hard. Many Transylvanian villagers still believe in strigoi, vârcolaci, witches, and the living dead. Romanian television often broadcasts call-in talk shows hosted by women claiming to be witches, who try and help people with their problems. Many people still visit fortune-tellers, who are often Roma women, and astrologers.

Vampires continue to be reported in the news in Romania. The nation was shocked by a case of vampirism becoming world news in 2004. In the village of Marotinu de Sus, a recently deceased man, Toma Petrica, was suspected of having become a strigoi. His relatives dug up his body and removed the heart, which was burned and the ashes given as medicine to those who claimed to have been made ill by the strigoi. Local authorities were upset by the bad publicity, which came just as Romania was preparing for membership in the European Union. Eventually, the family was fined and made to pay for damages to the cemetery.

In 2008, a case of vampirism was reported concerning a Muslim Roma woman, Ghiulten Memedali, in the city of Medgidia. Memedali's corpse was found with its heart removed after a family dispute. And in nearby Serbia, where the original wampyr scares originated in the 1720s, a vampire sighting was reported in the village of Jablanica in September

Roma women still find a steady demand for their services as fortune-tellers in modern Romania. Belief in fortune-telling and supernatural events is still strong in cities, as well as in the countryside.

2009. According to Serbian television and newspapers, a vampire stalked the village at night, scratching at walls, breaking glass, and scaring dogs and animals. A priest was called in to calm the vampire down. However, some of the villagers began carrying grass in their belts believing that it could keep the vampire away.

A lingering hint of magic still influences public life in Romania to this day. After the 2009 presidential election, losing candidate Mircea Geoană publicly accused the winner, President Traian Băsescu, of using "the power of purple flame" to influence the outcome of the election and surrounding himself with "people with known paranormal abilities."

TRANSYLVANIA TODAY

In Transylvania today, the old ways exist comfortably alongside the new. Modern shopping malls and business centers fill the cities, while horse carts still bring produce to city markets. Many villagers still wear traditional folk costume on Sundays. At weddings, people still dance to traditional violin bands, as well as to the latest international hip-hop hits. More people

TRANSYLVANIAN FOOD

Transylvanian cuisine contains a great deal of meat, especially fatty smoked bacon, which is cut in thick slabs and eaten raw with bread for lunch. Skinless meatball sausages grilled outdoors, called *mititei* or *mici*, are popular at open-air marketplaces. A simple cornmeal porridge, called *mamaliga*, is a staple of Transylvanian food. Sometimes cooked with the water left over from cheesemaking and called *balmus*, it is served with salty sheep cheese or stew. Transylvanian food plays a role in Bram Stoker's novel *Dracula*: the second paragraph of the book describes a meal of spicy paprika chicken, or *csirke paprikás*, a Hungarian dish well known throughout Transylvania.

now watch cable television in their villages than listen to mythical stories of vârcolaci and strigoi. One of the most isolated nations in Europe under Communism, Romania has since opened up to the world.

Transylvanians still hold large peasant fairs of a kind rarely seen anymore in Europe. Traditionally, fairs were a chance for people living in different areas to meet and trade and, especially, find a marriage partner. The most traditional of these fairs takes place on the second weekend of October in the Transylvanian mountain town of Negreni. Thousands of people gather in Negreni to attend the fair, which is filled with people bargaining in all languages of the Transylvanian hills: Romanian, Hungarian, and Romani. Vendor stalls sell folk costumes, farm tools, and

The Gabor tribe of Roma Gypsies work as coppersmiths and sell household goods at fairs around Transylvania. They are identifiable by the wide-brimmed black hats worn by the men and the colorful skirts worn by the women.

antiques—but none of the Dracula souvenirs that can be found in tourist shops in the towns. Even as the Negreni fair becomes more modern, it reminds Transylvanians that change is creeping into their mountains faster than anyone ever suspected. How long can the familiar past and the beckoning future coexist before one overshadows the other?

Few places in Europe have been able to maintain such a vibrant traditional life as in this mountainous corner of Romania. Much of the world knows Transylvania only through the fictional world of vampire books and movies. This horror-story image of Transylvania has been so powerful that the real Transylvania has almost become invisible. The real Transylvania—with its tall wooden churches, storybook villages, and "happy cemeteries"—has its own story to tell. As more people visit this beautiful land, with its rich history and friendly people, the story of Transylvania will grow beyond the realm of vampires.

Timeline

c. 105

Rome conquers the Dacians.

451

Fall of Rome; the empire continues in the east as Byzantium.

896

Magyar tribes led by King Arpad conquer Transylvania and incorporate it into the Hungarian crown.

1054

The Great Schism occurs. Catholic and Eastern Orthodox Christian churches divide into two religions.

1389

Serb armies lose to Turkish forces at the Battle of Kosovo.

1453

Constantinople falls to the Ottoman Turks.

1456

The Ottoman Empire is defeated by John Hunyadi at Belgrade, Serbia. Vlad Tepes takes control of Walachia.

1476

Death of Vlad Tepes.

1526

Turks defeat the Hungarian king at the Battle of Mohács. Transylvania becomes an Ottoman vassal state.

1610

Transylvanian princess Elizabeth Báthory is convicted of mass murder.

1700

Transylvania is incorporated into the Habsburg Empire.

1727

Arnold Paole, a Habsburg soldier, is reported to be a vampire.

1732

Doctor Johann Flückinger publishes *Visum et Reportum*, Europe's first major vampire report. A vampire literature craze hits Europe.

1816

Lord Byron's friend John Polidori writes the first English vampire novel.

1847

Bram Stoker, author of *Dracula*, is born in Dublin, Ireland.

1890

In the library of Whitby, England, Stoker names the character of his new novel Dracula.

1897

Dracula is published to wide success.

1912

Bram Stoker dies.

1918

Transylvania becomes part of the Kingdom of Romania.

1922

Nosferatu premieres in Berlin.

1931

Transylvanian actor Bela Lugosi plays Count Dracula in the film *Dracula*.

1945

Transylvanian territories are returned to Romania after World War II. An era of Communist government begins.

1989

The Romanian Revolution ends the Communist era.

2004

Romania enters the European Union just as another vampire scandal breaks out in the village of Marotinu de Sus.

2009

Romanian politicians accuse each other of using supernatural forces to win the presidential election.

GLOSSARY

anthropologist A social scientist who studies human cultures.

assimilate To absorb and integrate into a people or culture.

astrology The study of the movements and relative positions of celestial bodies and their supposed influence on human affairs.

boyar A high-ranking noble in Romania or Russia prior to the twentieth century.

byzantium The Eastern Roman Empire during the Middle Ages.

coexist To exist in harmony.

Communism A political and social system whereby all property is owned by the community.

consecrate To make or declare sacred.

erratic Not regular in pattern or movement.

exhume To dig out something buried, especially a corpse, from the ground.

feudal system The dominant social system in medieval Europe, in which the nobility held lands owned by the crown in exchange for military service, and vassals were tenants of and protected by the nobles.

folklore The traditional beliefs, stories, and customs of a community, passed on by word of mouth.

Gothic literature A story that combines themes of both romance and horror.

impalement A kind of execution where someone is pierced with a large wooden stake.

incantation Words spoken as a magic spell or charm.

linguist A person who studies languages.

nationalism A political movement based on patriotic feeling, often to an excessive degree.

nomad A member of a group of people who have no permanent home and are continually moving to find fresh pasture for their animals.

Ottoman Empire An Islamic empire led by Turkish sultans that existed between the thirteenth and twentieth centuries.

paranormal abilities Mental states supposedly beyond the scope of normal scientific understanding.

plagiarism To take the work or idea of someone else and pass it off as one's own.

Romanticism A movement in which artists rebelled against the careful, scientific description of relationships and instead sought to describe extreme emotional states of love, horror, or awe.

vassal A person or country in a subordinate position to another.

Vlachs A once nomadic ethnic group of the Balkans descended from Roman settlers. The Vlachs spoke Romance languages related to Romanian.

Open Society Institute and Soros Foundation Network

400 West 59th Street

New York, NY 10019

(212) 548-0600

Web site: http://www.soros.org

The Open Society Institute is dedicated to promoting democracy and fairness in government. Its Soros Foundations are established in individual countries to carry out this work. Soros Foundation Romania focuses on critical issues for the development of Romanian society and is dedicated to the development of Romania's human resources in culture, education, and human rights.

Romanian Association of Canada

2210 Predeal Trudeau

Val David, QC J0T-2N0

Canada

Web site: http://www.arcanada.org/english/index.html

This association assists Romanian immigrants and sponsors cultural events for one of North America's largest Romanian communities.

Romanian Culture Institute New York

200 East 38th Street

New York, NY 10016

(212) 687-0180

Web site: http://www.icrny.org/index.html

The Romanian Culture Institute has a long history of supporting Romanian arts and culture. It also has an extensive library and many resources for research.

Romanian National Tourist Office

355 Lexington Avenue, 8th Floor

New York, NY 10017

(212) 545-8484

Web site: http://www.romaniatourism.com
The Romanian National Tourist Office is the official representative of the
Romanian Ministry of Tourism in the United States and Canada. Its Web
site offers extensive information on many aspects of culture, history, and
Dracula lore in Transylvania.

Transylvania Society of Dracula

Canadian Chapter

2309-397 Front Street West

Toronto, ON M5V 3S1

Canada

Web site: http://www.ucs.mun.ca/~emiller
The Transylvania Society of Dracula is an international organization, based
in Romania, dedicated to the study of Dracula and vampires in Romania.
North Americans can refer to the Canadian chapter, led by Dracula educa-
tor and author Elizabeth Miller.

WEB SITES

Due to the changing nature of Internet links, Rosen Publishing has
developed an online list of Web sites related to the subject of this book.
This site is updated regularly. Please use this link to access the list:

http://www.rosenlinks.com/vamp/tbov

Barber, Paul. *Vampires, Burial, and Death: Folklore and Reality*. Hartford, CT: Yale University Press, 1988.

Bartlett, Wayne, and Flavia Idriceanu. *Legends of Blood: The Vampire in History and Myth*. Santa Barbara, CA: Praeger Publishers, 2006.

Bibeau, Paul. *Sundays with Vlad: From Pennsylvania to Transylvania, One Man's Quest to Live in the World of the Undead*. New York, NY: Three Rivers Press, 2007.

Codrescu, Andrei. *The Blood Countess*. New York, NY: Simon & Schuster, 1995.

Codrescu, Andrei. *The Hole in the Flag: A Romanian Exile's Story of Return and Revolution*. New York, NY: William Morrow, 1991.

Day, Peter, ed. *Vampires: Myths and Metaphors of Enduring Evil*. Amsterdam, Holland: Editions Rodopi, 2006.

Dundes, Alan, ed. *The Vampire: A Casebook*. Madison, WI: University of Wisconsin Press, 1998.

Fonseca, Isabel. *Bury Me Standing: The Gypsies and Their Journey*. New York, NY: Knopf, 1995.

Jokai, Mor (Maurus). *The Golden Age in Transylvania*. Amsterdam, Holland: Fredonia Books: 2004.

Kaplan, Robert D. *Balkan Ghosts: A Journey Through History*. New York, NY: Picador, 2005.

Kast, Sheilah, and Jim Rosapepe. *Dracula Is Dead*. Hollywood, FL: Bancroft Press, 2009.

Keper, Nicolai. *Romania: An Illustrated History*. New York, NY: Hippocrene Books, 2004.

Keyworth, David. *Troublesome Corpses: Vampires & Revenants, from Antiquity to the Present*. Southend-on-Sea, England: Desert Island Books, Ltd., 2007.

Leland, Charles Geofrey. *Gypsy Sorcery and Fortune Telling: Illustrated by Incantations, Specimens of Medical Magic, Anecdotes, and Tales*. New York, NY: Citadel Press, 1990.

McNally, Raymond T., and Radu Florescu. *In Search of Dracula: The History of Dracula and Vampires*. New York, NY: Houghton Mifflin, 1994.

Miller, Elizabeth. *Bram Stoker's Dracula: A Documentary Journey into Vampire Country and the Dracula Phenomenon*. New York, NY: Pegasus Books, 2009.

Miller, Elizabeth. *Dracula: Sense and Nonsense*. Westcliff-on-Sea, England: Desert Island Books, 2000.

Stoker, Bram. *Dracula*. New York, NY: W. W. Norton & Company, 1996.

Summers, Montague. *The Vampire in Lore and Legend*. Mineola, NY: Dover Publications, 2001.

Trow, M. J. *Vlad the Impaler: In Search of the Real Dracula*. Stroud, England: The History Press, 2004.

Andras, Carmen Maria. "The Image of Transylvania in English
    Literature." *Journal of Dracula Studies*, No.1, 1999. Retrieved
    December 20, 2009 (http://www.blooferland.com/drc/index.
    php?title=Journal_of_Dracula_Studies).

Blair, Justin, and Matthew Vincent. *Across the Forest*. DVD. 2009.

Codrescu, Andrei. *The Hole in the Flag: A Romanian Exile's Story of
    Return and Revolution*. New York, NY: William Morrow, 1991.

"Conspiracy Theory: Bizarre Claims of Malicious 'Energy Attacks'
    Spark Mockery of Romanian Politics." HotNews.ro., January 18,
    2010. Retrieved January 25, 2010 (http://english.hotnews.ro/
    stiri-top_news-6825685-conspiracy-theory-bizarre-claims-malicious-
    energy-attacks-spark-mockery-romanian-politics.htm).

Crisan, Marius. "The Models for Castle Dracula in Stoker's Sources on
    Transylvania." *Journal of Dracula Studies*, No. 10, 2008. Retrieved
    December 20, 2009 (http://www.blooferland.com/drc/index.
    php?title=Journal_of_Dracula_Studies).

Dundes, Alan, ed. *The Vampire: A Casebook*. Madison, WI: University of
    Wisconsin Press, 1998.

Johnson, Patrick. "Count Dracula and the Folkloric Vampire: Thirteen
    Comparisons." *Journal of Dracula Studies*, No. 13, 2001. Retrieved
    December 20, 2009 (http://www.blooferland.com/drc/index.
    php?title=Journal_of_Dracula_Studies).

Kligman, Gail. *Calus: Symbolic Transformation in Romanian Ritual*.
    Chicago, IL: University of Chicago Press, 1981.

Kligman, Gail. *The Wedding of the Dead: Ritual, Poetics, and Popular
    Culture in Transylvania*. Berkeley, CA: University of California
    Press, 1990.

Kreuter, Peter Mario. "The Name of the Vampire: Some Reflections on Current Linguistic Theories on the Etymology of the Word Vampire." *Vampires: Myths and Metaphors of Enduring Evil*. Peter Day, ed. Amsterdam, Holland: Rodopi, 2006.

Light, Duncan. "The People of Bram Stoker's Transylvania." *Journal of Dracula Studies*, No. 7, 2005. Retrieved December 20, 2009 (http://www.blooferland.com/drc/index. php?title=Journal_of_Dracula_Studies).

McNally, Raymond T., and Radu Florescu. *In Search of Dracula: The History of Dracula and Vampires*. New York, NY: Houghton Mifflin, 1994.

Miller, Elizabeth. *Bram Stoker's Dracula: A Documentary Journey into Vampire Country and the Dracula Phenomenon*. New York, NY: Pegasus Books, 2009.

Mulligan, Tom. "Death Rite Unnerves Romanian EU Bid." BBC News, March 5, 2004. Retrieved February 2, 2010 (http://news.bbc.co.uk/2/ hi/europe/3537085.stm).

Murgoci, Agnes. "The Vampire in Roumania." *The Vampire: A Casebook*. Alan Dundes, ed. Madison, WI: University of Wisconsin Press, 1998.

Rezachevici, Constantin. "From the Order of the Dragon to Dracula." *Journal of Dracula Studies*, No. 1, 1999. Retrieved December 20, 2009 (http://www.blooferland.com/drc/index. php?title=Journal_of_Dracula_Studies).

Stoker, Bram. *Dracula*. New York, NY: W. W. Norton & Company, 1996.

INDEX

ABOUT THE AUTHOR

Robert Z. Cohen is a writer, folklorist, and musician who has spent more than twenty years traveling throughout southeast Europe as both a journalist and editor (*Budapest Week*, *Hungary Report*, and *Hungarian Spectator*) and travel guide writer (*TimeOut! Budapest* and *Fodor's Guides*.) Born in New York City and educated as an anthropologist and linguist, Cohen has recorded folk music among many of east Europe's diverse communities. He performs Transylvanian-style Jewish Klezmer music on the fiddle with his band, Di Naye Kapelye. He lives in Budapest, Hungary.

PHOTO CREDITS

Designer: Les Kanturek;
Photo Researcher: Amy Feinberg